Let's Talk to God Again
by Zinnia Bryan

Illustrated by
Carolyn Dinan

SCRIPTURE UNION
47 Marylebone Lane, London, W1M 6AX

Printed in Great Britain by Hazell Watson & Viney Ltd,
Aylesbury, Bucks

CONTENTS

WHEN YOU PRAY, SAY....

OUR FATHER WHO ART IN HEAVEN

God our Father, we thank you for making and giving us all that we need for life on this earth. We thank you for water: for the Atlantic Ocean where the big ships sail, and for water in our taps at home. We thank you for swimming pools and puddles, streams and ponds, ice-cubes in orange juice and water to wash with.

In Jesus' Name. Amen.

Heavenly Father, you have made the whole world, and everyone living in it belongs to you. All the families of the earth are in your care. Thank you that that every person on earth is known to you and loved. We remember that you want everyone to love and obey you. Thank you that you do not force people to follow you. We ask in Jesus' Name that the peoples of the world may come to love and praise you. Amen.

Father God, we thank you for all the good things you *give* us because you love us. For friends and animals and food, we thank you. For balls and books and the fun of laughing, we thank you.

But even more we thank you for all the things you *do* because you love us. For always keeping your promises, for caring when we are sad, for being ready to forgive when we are sorry, we thank you.

And most of all, for sending Jesus to die for our sins and come alive again, we thank you.

In his Name. Amen.

Dear God, you are my heavenly Father and I am your child. You love me and want to teach me how to grow like you. You are my keeper. You never leave me or get tired of looking after me. Thank you. Help me to love you more and to be obedient to you.

For Jesus' sake. Amen.

Heavenly Father, we praise you, for you are great and strong. You made the highest mountain in the world, and also the hill nearest our home. We thank you for the excitement of high places. We thank you, too, for legs to climb with and eyes to see the view. Amen.

HALLOWED BE THY NAME

Dear God, please teach us how important you are and how important your Name is. Help us to remember that it is the most important Name in all the world. Please keep us from using it wrongly. Help us not to say your Name unless we are thinking about you.

For Jesus' sake. Amen.

Lord Jesus, we are glad that God has given you a Name which is greater than any other name. We know that one day everyone will kneel at your Name and worship you as God. We praise you, Lord Jesus. Amen.

Lord our God, you are so great and wonderful that even your Name is special. May the whole world kneel down to you. May everyone say, 'The Lord is King'. We pray for the people who do not know you and for those who laugh at your Name, thinking it does not matter. Help us all to understand that you are the living God. Amen.

Lord Jesus, we pray for the people who write books and plays and act on television and in films. Thank you for the enjoyment that they give us. May they honour you, using your Name in the right way only.

For your sake. Amen.

Lord Jesus Christ, you have said that if we ask anything in your Name, you will do it. Thank you for this promise. Help us to obey you always, loving you more than anyone.

In your Name. Amen.

THY KINGDOM COME

O Lord our God, your Kingdom comes when people are ready to have you as King. We want you to be our King. Help us to find out what you want us to do, and then do it. Help us to love you, to talk to you, to put you first before ourselves and others, and to believe the things you tell us in the Bible. Thank you for sending the Lord Jesus to open the way for us into your Kingdom.

In his Name. Amen.

Lord Jesus, our Saviour, you have said, 'Let the children come to me and do not stop them; for to such belongs the Kingdom of God'. Thank you that we may belong to you. We pray for the children of the world. May they hear the good news of your love for them. May they come to know and follow you, obeying your rules and believing your promises.

In your Name we pray. Amen.

Heavenly Father, we pray for the people who are working to teach children about you—in this country and in other countries, too. We think of those who run children's homes, Bible clubs and Sunday schools; those who write books, make films and broadcast over the radio; those who work in hospitals and schools, in faraway villages and big towns. Please help them to explain about you in a way that boys and girls can understand.

For Jesus' sake. Amen.

Dear God, help us to remember that most of the people in the world are *still* waiting to hear about Jesus. They are not in your Kingdom yet. We thank you that you love them and want them, too. We ask in Jesus' Name to send people to tell them of your love.

For his sake. Amen.

God our Father, we thank you that we have the Bible to read in our own language. We pray for those who have no Bible and for those who are working to put it into their language for them. Help them to find exactly the right words to give the real meaning of your message. We pray for the Bible Societies and for everyone who prints and sells and takes your Book to the people still without it. Please help them in their work.

For Jesus' sake. Amen.

O Lord, thank you for radio that reaches into places where missionaries cannot go. We pray for programmes broadcasting the good news of Jesus and explaining what the Bible says. Please help the people in charge of them. Give them good ideas and help them to send the programmes out clearly so that the people listening may hear and understand.

In Jesus' Name. Amen.

Loving Father, thank you that you know and love each person separately. Thank you that even in big crowds we cannot be lost from you. We pray for the thousands of people living in the big cities of the world. We pray for those who feel lonely and lost, for those who have uninteresting jobs with little pay, for those who live squashed up in crowded rooms. Especially we pray for the millions who do not know about you. Help those who work to tell them. Make them cheerful and friendly as they share the good news of your love. Help them to find the people who need you.

For Jesus' sake. Amen.

Heavenly Father, thank you for our church. Thank you that we may come each week to be together with you, to praise you, talk to you and listen to you. Help us as we meet together, to grow in our love for each other as we grow in our love for you. Help us not to keep you to ourselves but to share you with our friends and neighbours, so that this place where we live may become a place where you are known and honoured and obeyed.

In Jesus' Name. Amen.

Lord Jesus, please make yourself real to me. Teach me how to talk to you in my own words without needing a book. Help me to love you and believe you. Make me want to obey you so that your Kingdom may come in my heart. Amen.

THY WILL BE DONE

In the world

Great God our Father, we thank you that you are in charge of the whole world. We pray today for the leaders and rulers of every country. Please put good and kind thoughts into their minds. Help them to make right decisions so that the people living under them may be treated fairly. Help the leaders of the world to obey your rules so that everyone may live in peace without being afraid.

In the Name of Jesus. Amen.

In our country

Dear God, we pray for our country, for our Queen and Members of Parliament. Make them strong and brave to stand up for what is right. May they remember that you are the One in charge. Help them to lead our country in your ways. Help us all to hate wrong and to obey you, putting you first. Teach us to live together unselfishly and happily, ready to work hard and to give our best for each other.

In Jesus' Name. Amen.

In our school

Heavenly Father, may what you want, be done in our school today. Help us to work hard, remembering to finish carefully the things we begin. Help us to be kind and friendly, ready to lend and give. Make us helpful in the classroom, specially when it comes to the jobs that nobody likes. Be with us in our speaking that we may say only the things that are true and good.

For Jesus' sake. Amen.

11

In our homes

Be with us in our homes, Lord Jesus. Help us to make them places where you are put first. Make us obedient and polite to our Mothers and Fathers, as you were; friendly and unselfish with our brothers and sisters. Make us ready to share and to give—even when someone else wants what we want. Make us quick to help, even if we're watching our favourite programme on television. Help us to behave in a way that pleases you so that your will may be done in our homes. Amen.

Please, God, help me to do as I am told at home, at school, and when I am out. Help me to do it straightaway.
For Jesus' sake. Amen.

Lord Jesus, our Saviour, please help us to show that we love you by obeying you, for you have said, 'If you love me you will keep my commandments'. Amen.

Lord Jesus, when my friends try to persuade me to do something that you wouldn't like, please make me strong enough to say No. May I be ready to go your way even if they laugh at me.
In your Name I ask this. Amen.

O Lord my God, you have said, 'Children, obey your parents'. Please help me to keep this rule.
You have said, 'Be kind to one another'. Please help me to keep this rule.
You have said, 'Work hard and with gladness all the time as though working for Christ'. Please help me to keep this rule.
You have said, 'Call upon me in the day of trouble'. Please help me to keep this rule. Amen.

God, our Father, we thank you that in heaven your Name is honoured and your Kingdom has come, for everyone there obeys you and is glad that you are King. Please make it like that here on earth, specially in this place where we live.

For Jesus' sake. Amen.

———————

GIVE US THIS DAY OUR DAILY BREAD

Heavenly Father, every day I have the things I need: food to eat, clothes to wear, people to love, friends to play with, and a school where I can learn. Thank you for showing your love to me by all these things you give me. Amen.

Please, God, help us to remember that the milkman can only bring us milk because you have given us cows. We can only eat crisps because you have made potatoes. We can only watch television because you have given us eyes. We can only breathe because you have made the air and given us lungs. Help us to stop sometimes to remember that you keep us alive. Thank you for this interesting and exciting world that you have put us in. Amen.

Lord Jesus, you have said, 'Do not be worried about the food and drink you need to stay alive, or about clothes for your body. Your Father in heaven knows that you need these things'. Please help us to obey you. When we are worried, help us to tell you about it and really to believe that you are looking after us. Amen.

Thank you, Lord, that we do not have to wonder if we shall have anything to eat today. Thank you for our food and for our strong healthy bodies. Thank you for the people who cook for us. Help us to be grateful, eating our meals without fussiness or wasting. We have so much, Lord, please keep us from being greedy. Help us to think of ways in which we can share with those who have so little.

In Jesus' Name. Amen.

Lord Jesus, I have good meals each day, as well as biscuits in between and money to spend on sweets and crisps. There are children starving today. Please help me to help them by sometimes giving my pocket money to buy them food. Amen.

Thank you, Father, for the societies and people who are working for those who are hungry. Help us who live in rich countries to give gladly and often for their work. We pray for farmers teaching people better ways of growing food. We pray for doctors and nurses working to cure those who are ill with hunger. We pray for welfare workers teaching mothers the best foods to give their children. Be with these people as they work, Lord.

For Jesus' sake. Amen.

Thank you, dear God, for our safe and comfortable homes. Thank you for a place that belongs to us, and a family to share it with. Thank you that we have a place to go when it rains and when night comes. Thank you that we can keep warm inside it even in winter. We think of those who have no home of their own, who sleep in the streets and get wet when it rains and cold in the winter. Help us to care about them as much as you do. Help their countries to build flats and houses for them to live in.

We ask it in Jesus' Name, who sometimes had nowhere to sleep himself. Amen.

Thank you, Heavenly Father, for all the people working on farms and in mills and factories and shops to bring us clothes. Thank you for our own clothes and for the fun of shopping for new ones. Thank you for our Mothers who wash them and mend them. Thank you for washing machines and irons and all other things that help her look after them. We pray for those who are too poor to buy clothes for themselves. Help us to find ways of giving and sharing with them.

For Jesus' sake. Amen.

Dear God, we thank you for giving us Fathers and Mothers to look after us. We thank you that our Fathers are able to get jobs and earn money to buy us the things we need. We pray for all the fathers who are out of work today and cannot get a job. Please help them to find work and help their countries to provide jobs for them.

In Jesus' Name. Amen.

FORGIVE US OUR TRESPASSES

Dear God, you have said, 'Love the Lord your God with all your heart'. I have not loved you with all my heart. Please forgive me. Help me to get to know you better and grow to love you more.

In Jesus' Name. Amen.

Lord Jesus, you always do things well. Please forgive us for the times we have done wrong by being careless. We are sorry for the work we didn't finish, the 'thank you' we forgot to say, the friend we didn't help, the quarrel we didn't make up. Please help us to be thoughtful and thorough like you. Amen.

Thoughts

Dear God, you have given us minds to think with, but so often out thoughts are not right or good.

For when we have thought we were better than others, we are sorry, Lord.

For when we have thought it wasn't fair we didn't get first turn, we are sorry, Lord.

For when we have specially remembered the things we don't like about someone, we are sorry, Lord.

For when we have been jealous, wishing we had something that belonged to someone else, we are sorry, Lord.

For when we have planned something wrong to do, we are sorry, Lord.

Please forgive us, for Jesus' sake. Amen.

Words

Please, Heavenly Father, forgive us for the times we have hurt you by what we have said. For when we have told lies, said unkind things about others, quarrelled with our friends and told tales on them, we are sorry. We thank you that because of the Lord Jesus you are able to forgive us. Amen.

Lord Jesus, I am sorry for when I have whined to get my own way, or made others miserable by moaning and complaining. Please forgive me and help me always to speak cheerfully.

For your sake. Amen.

Lord Jesus Christ, we have sometimes been rude to our parents and teachers. We have answered back when we have been told off. We have been impolite and cheeky to people we have met. We are sorry. Please forgive us, for you died to take away our sins. Amen.

Deeds

Dear Father God, we are sorry for our selfish behaviour. Please forgive us for pushing and barging to get in front, for treading on people's toes and sometimes even knocking them over. Please forgive us for snatching things away from people smaller than ourselves and for breaking things that did not belong to us. Please help us to be gentle and kind as Jesus is.

For his sake. Amen.

O God, we cannot hide from you the wrong things we do. You know when we disobey, take things that do not belong to us, and hurt our friends. Please forgive us and help us to hate these wrong things as much as you do.

For Jesus' sake. Amen.

AS WE FORGIVE THOSE WHO TRESPASS AGAINST US

We thank you, loving God, that when we come to say sorry, you are always ready to forgive. Please help us to be like you. When people say sorry to us may we forgive them straightaway, ready at once to be friends again.

In Jesus' Name. Amen.

Heavenly Father, thank you that when you forgive the wrong things we do, you forget about them, too, for you have said, 'I will not remember your sins'. May we be the same. Help us to forget the wrong things people do to us.

For your Names' sake. Amen.

Father God, help us to be unselfish, ready to give and lend and share, willing to spend our time on other people, even when they themselves are selfish. Amen.

People who are unkind to me

Father God, you know about the people who are unkind to me. Please help me not to be unkind back. Help us to be friends.

For Jesus' sake. Amen.

People I do not like

Lord Jesus, I pray today for the people I do not like. Help me to be kind and friendly to them. Thank you for loving them as much as me. Help me to have your kind of love for them. Amen.

My Family

Heavenly Father, you made the first family. Thank you for my family. Thank you for giving me my Father and Mother and my brothers and sisters. Thank you for my home. May it be a place where I learn to be patient and forgiving, slow to fight back and quick to be friends. May we learn to love and follow you as a family together. Amen.

The people around us

Dear God, we pray for the people we know, and for those who help us by the work they do: our next door neighbours; the people at the library; those who work in television; shop assistants and factory workers. They all help to make life good for us. Especially we thank you for our friends. Please help us to be polite, ready to help and to forgive, remembering that you are the one God and Father of us all.

In Jesus' Name. Amen.

Newcomers

Please, God, make me friendly and welcoming to the newcomers I meet, ready to look after them and settle them in. Help me to know what to talk about, specially if they are shy and don't know what to say.

For Jesus' sake. Amen.

Strangers

Father God, we think of all the people living near us who are strangers to us. We thank you that they are not strangers to you. If they are lonely, please comfort them. If they have troubles and difficulties, help them. If they do not believe in you please show yourself to them, so that they may know that you are the living God who loves them and wants them.

In Jesus' Name. Amen.

LEAD US NOT INTO TEMPTATION

Please, Heavenly Father, help us today, for we need you. We want to please you but we cannot be good without your help. Please keep us from doing wrong, and make us able to do what is right.

In Jesus' Name we pray. Amen.

Dear God, we thank you for the voice inside that tells us when something is wrong. Please teach us to hear it quickly. Make us ready to obey it.

For Jesus' sake. Amen.

O Lord our God, we are glad that you are so strong. Please keep Satan from putting wrong ideas into our heads. Please keep us from turning wrong ideas into thoughts and wrong thoughts into wrong things to do.

For Jesus' sake we ask it. Amen.

God our Father, we love you and we are on your side against wrong. Please help us to be strong for you, knowing that Jesus is with us to give us his strength. Amen.

Loving Father, you know me through and through. You know the wrong things that I cannot stop doing. Please help me today. I cannot keep myself from doing wrong. Please will you keep me.
For Jesus' sake. Amen.

Dear God, please take away from me the love of doing wrong. Help me not to *want* to do it. Help me not to think it is funny, or clever, or unimportant. Help me to hate sin as much as you do.
For Jesus' sake. Amen.

Lord Jesus, thank you for dying to take away my sin. Thank you for coming alive again to keep me from sin. Thank you that you are with me every day to make me strong, and that all the time you are praying to God for me. Amen.

Lord Jesus, when Satan tries to make me frightened, help me to remember that you are with me keeping me safe. When he tries to make me worried, help me to remember that you are looking after me and that you are stronger than him. Amen.

Father God, we thank you that if we sin you are able to forgive us, because the Lord Jesus has died and come alive again for us. Amen.

Dear God, please keep me from being grumpy and help me not to sulk. When someone shouts at me help me not to shout back. When someone hits me help me not to hit back.
In the Name of the Lord Jesus. Amen.

Dear God, thank you for the Bible which is your word to us. Help us to read it and get to know it so that we may not sin against you. Teach us how to use it as Jesus did, when Satan comes to tempt us.

In his Name we pray this. Amen.

Dear Lord, please keep us from being lazy and too easily put off. When we want to give up before the end of a job help us to keep at it until we finish. Help us to make the end as good as the beginning. For Jesus' sake, who finished the work you gave him to do. Amen.

BUT DELIVER US FROM EVIL

Deliver us from not loving
Church Unity

Dear God, please keep your people from quarrelling and splitting up. Please fill your whole Church with love for you. Give us your love for each other so that all the world may know that we are Jesus' followers.

In his Name we pray. Amen.

(*The whole Church is not the building you go to on Sunday, but everyone who loves and belongs to the Lord Jesus.*)

Unhappy Homes

Father God, it is not your will that families should break up with fights and arguments. You mean us to live together in love and happiness. We pray for the families where people are in trouble with each other and are living in sadness and hate. Help them to be loving and understanding, ready to forgive and to put each other first. Especially we ask you to comfort all those who are sad and troubled because they cannot live together any more. Help them to find you and your love.

In Jesus' Name. Amen.

We praise you, Heavenly Father, for making the people of the world so different and yet so alike. We thank you that each of us is a special person wonderfully made and loved by you. Thank you for giving us so much to share with each other. Please help us to remember that whatever language we speak, whatever country we come from, whatever colour our skin is, we are all as important to you. Please keep us from being un-loving to each other.

In Jesus' Name who gave himself for everyone. Amen.

War

O Lord our God, we are glad that you are still in charge of this troubled world. So many people are sad because of war. So many have been hurt and made afraid. So many have lost their homes and the people they love. Please show *your* love to them, we pray. And, Father God, you are the One who makes wars end in all the earth. Please take away from us our hating and cruelty. Give us hearts that love and thoughts that are kind. Make the day come quickly when everybody on earth shall know who you are.

In Jesus' Name. Amen.

The Elderly

Lord Jesus, we remember today the old people living around us. Especially we think of those who are lonely and poor and have no one to visit them or take them out. Please help us not to forget them. Thank you for all that they have done for us. Help them to know that you are the Friend who never leaves us nor forgets us. Amen.

Deliver us from illness

For Doctors, nurses and dentists

Dear God, we thank you for the work of all doctors and nurses and other medical people. We thank you for our hospitals. We thank you for all those who work there—the porters, the cooks, the cleaners and lots of others. We ask you to give the surgeons and nurses steady and gentle hands. We pray for our own doctor. Help him as he works to make his patients well again. Thank you for his help to us. We thank you, too, for the dentist and for all that he does to keep our teeth strong and healthy. We thank you for the district nurse and the health visitor and for all the help and comfort they bring to our families. We thank you for the chemist who provides us with medicines and the scientists who are working to find new cures. Help us all to remember that it is you who gives us healing.

In Jesus' Name. Amen.

Those who have no doctor

We thank you, Father, that when we are ill we can go to the doctor and get medicine. We pray for the thousands of people in the world who have no doctor near them and no medicine. We pray for more doctors and nurses in these places, and hospitals, too. We ask you to help those who are already there, specially when they are tired and overworked.

In Jesus' Name. Amen.

Those who are ill

Lord Jesus Christ, we pray for all who are ill today. Please help them to get better. If they are in pain, comfort and ease them. If they are frightened help them to know that you are with them. Make them brave. If they have been ill a long time, encourage them and help them to be cheerful. Specially we pray for the people we know who are ill . . . . We thank you that you love to heal. Please make them well again soon. Amen.

The disabled

God, our loving Father, we pray for the people who cannot live an ordinary life like us: for those who are blind or deaf or unable to move. Thank you for their bravery and cheerfulness. Please comfort and help them. Be specially near them as they struggle to do things we find easy. May they know that you love them and care for them.

In Jesus' Name. Amen.

For myself

Thank you, God, that I am well and strong. Thank you that I can run and skip and climb, that I can see and hear and use my hands. Please keep me safe from illness and accident.

In Jesus' Name. Amen.

25

Those who are depressed

We thank you, Loving Father, that we can praise you because you care for us. We pray for the people who are worried and feeling miserable or ill in their minds. Please help the doctors and nurses and families looking after them to be understanding. Please make them better, Lord. Comfort them and teach them to give their worries to you. Help us, too, to tell you about our worries and troubles, knowing that you will look after us.

In Jesus' Name. Amen.

Deliver us from danger

Road safety

Lord Jesus, please keep me safe on the roads. Help me to remember and obey the Highway Code, both when I am on my bicycle and when I am walking. Amen.

Thank you, God, for the fun of travelling. Thank you for jets and helicopters, liners and yachts, for rockets and space-craft, underground trains and escalators; for cars and trains, scooters and lorries.

Please watch over all who travel today. Give them common sense and politeness. Teach them to guard against accidents, and to obey the rules made for their safety.

In Jesus' Name. Amen.

Home safety

Heavenly Father, we ask you to keep us safe in our homes. Please guard us from fire and accident. Help us to be careful with cookers and irons and other electrical things. Keep us from using tools and medicines, glass and knives carelessly or in the wrong way.

In Jesus' Name. Amen.

People whose work is dangerous

Dear God, we pray today for the people whose work is dangerous: for those who build skyscrapers, bridges, tunnels and railways; for those who knock down old buildings or cut down enormous trees; for fishermen and sailors battling with stormy seas; for soldiers and airmen; for men in factories working with powerful machines; for coal miners, spacemen and circus people; for policemen, watchmen and firemen; and for all others who are in danger through their work. Please keep them from accident, we pray.

In Jesus' Name. Amen.

Deliver us from living without God

O Lord our God, we pray for our country, for our homes and schools and the places where our Fathers work. We pray for our shops and cinemas and libraries. Help us to make them places where you would be welcome. Help us not to forget you, and please keep us from the troubles and unhappiness that come when your rules are disobeyed.

We pray in Jesus' Name. Amen.

Lord Jesus, I bring to you the bad habits I have that I cannot break. Thank you that you can break them. Help me as I grow up to form good habits, not bad ones, and to live each day sharing it with you.

I ask this in your Name. Amen.

FOR THINE IS THE KINGDOM THE POWER AND THE GLORY FOR EVER AND EVER

We give thanks to you, O Lord God, for you are good. The things you do are always right. The words you speak are always true. We give thanks to you, for you are King. Your Kingdom is wonderful and lasts for ever. You are always in charge. Every day your love and kindness are the same. You give us food to eat and all we need to live. You are gentle and loving with everything you have made.

We give thanks to you, for you are our God and we belong to you.

In Jesus' Name. Amen.

God, our loving Father, thank you that you never change. You are as strong and wise and loving as the day you made the world. Thank you that nothing can ever happen that will make you alter. You are the one true God and Maker of all. We worship you in Jesus' Name. Amen.

Heavenly Father, we thank you that you listen to us when we talk to you.

In Jesus' Name. Amen.

THE LORD JESUS

THE LORD JESUS OUR FRIEND AND LEADER

The wedding at Cana.—St. John 2. 1–11

Lord Jesus, thank you for changing the water into wine. Thank you for showing us that you care about our happiness. Help us to make room for you in all that we do, especially in the happy things, and teach us to take Mary's advice to do whatever you tell us.

In your Name we pray. Amen.

The rich young man.—St. Mark 10. 17–22

Lord Jesus, you loved the rich young man and wanted him to follow you. We are sorry that he went away. Please keep us from being like him. Help us not to have anything in our lives that we want more than you.

In your Name. Amen.

Lord Jesus Christ, we thank you for the way you always went to help people when they asked. You went to Jairus' daughter, and the centurion's servant. You went to Lazarus, too. We thank you, Lord, that you never fail us, either. We thank you that when we call to you for help you always come to us. Amen.

Choosing Peter and Andrew —St. Mark 1. 16–20

Dear Lord Jesus Christ, thank you for choosing ordinary people in ordinary jobs to be your helpers. Thank you for choosing fishermen like Peter and Andrew and James and John. Thank you for loving them as they were, faults and all. Thank you for changing them and making them like yourself. We are ordinary people, too. We are glad that we may be your followers. Please make us like yourself.

In your Name. Amen.

Choosing James and John—St. Mark 1. 16–20

Jesus, our Lord, we thank you for the example of people like James and John. They left everything to follow you. We thank you that ever since then there have been men and women ready to leave everything for your sake. May we be willing to do the same.

In your Name we ask it. Amen.

Choosing Matthew—St. Mark 2. 13–14

We praise you, Lord Jesus, for calling even the people nobody liked, to be your helpers. Thank you for wanting Matthew. Help us to follow you as gladly as he did.

For your sake. Amen.

Zacchaeus—St. Luke 19. 1–10

Lord Jesus, thank you for knowing about Zacchaeus and caring for him. Thank you for loving him and changing him. Thank you that he wanted to see you so much he was even ready to climb a tree in spite of what others might think. Help us to want you as much as he did.

For your sake we ask it. Amen.

Jesus blesses the children—St. Mark 10. 13–16

Lord Jesus, you wanted the children to come and you blessed them all, not leaving anyone out. We thank you that you are never too busy to welcome us, and that you never leave anyone out. Please show us how to belong to your Kingdom.

For your sake. Amen.

Jesus and Peter—*St. Mark 16. 7*

Thank you, Lord Jesus, for understanding and caring how Peter felt. Thank you for specially mentioning his name so that he would know you forgave him and still wanted him, in spite of the awful thing he had done. Thank you for understanding our feelings and for wanting us, even when we let you down.

Amen.

Jesus' Friends—*St. John 15. 12–15*

Dear Lord Jesus, thank you for calling us your friends. Thank you for choosing us and sharing with us the things God shared with you. Help us to show that we are your true friends by doing what you tell us. You have said that the greatest love a man can have for his friends is to give his life for them. Thank you for giving your life for us.
Amen.

Jesus Christ the same for ever—*Hebrews 13. 8*

Lord Jesus, my Friend and Leader, I thank you that you never change. You welcome me when I come to you. You hear me when I talk to you. You forgive me when I say sorry to you. You help me when I call to you. You teach me when I listen to you. You lead me when I follow you. Help me to love you, to trust in you and to grow like you.

For your sake. Amen.

THE LORD JESUS OUR HEALER

Blind Bartimaeus—St. Mark 10. 46–52

Lord Jesus, we are glad that you didn't think Bartimaeus was just a noisy, unimportant beggar. Thank you for hearing him and making him able to see. Thank you that everybody is important to you, and that you hear all who call to you for help. Teach us to be like Bartimaeus, ready to go on praying till we have your answer.

In your Name. Amen.

The paralysed man—St. Mark 2. 1–12

We are glad, Lord Jesus, that you are able to forgive sins. Thank you for proving it by making the paralysed man well again. Thank you for knowing what he needed most of all. Thank you for knowing what we need most of all. Help us to understand that it is not only our bodies that need to be made well, but that you can cure us of our bad tempers, our lying and our naughtiness.

For your sake. Amen.

The man with the crippled hand—St. Luke 6. 6–11

Thank you, Lord Jesus, for being ready to heal the man's hand even though you knew it would get you into trouble with the Pharisees. Thank you for being so strong and brave. Thank you for the loving way you always put others first before yourself. Please make us ready to be unselfish and kind even when others do not understand.

For your sake. Amen.

The deaf and dumb man—St. Mark 7. 31–37

We thank you, Lord Jesus, for your kindness and thoughtfulness. You took the deaf and dumb man away to a quiet place and showed him what you were doing. Thank you for making him well. Thank you for doing *all* things well. Amen.

The widow's son at Nain—St. Luke 7. 11–17

Lord Jesus Christ, you never passed by anyone in need or trouble, and you were always able to help. You stopped at Nain when you saw the widow, and you were even able to make her son come alive again. We praise you, Lord Jesus, and we are glad that you are still the same today. You will never pass us by when we need help. You are able to deal with every difficulty we may have. Thank you. Amen.

The boy with the dumb spirit—St. Mark 9. 14–29

Lord Jesus, we are like the father of the sick boy. We do believe you are able to do wonderful things, but our faith is weak. Help us to grow strong in our believing. Help us to expect you to do great things for us today. We join in that father's prayer and say 'We do believe; help us to believe more'. Thank you for making his son well again. Amen.

The ten lepers—St. Luke 17. 11–19

We are sorry, Lord Jesus, that only one out of the ten lepers remembered to say thank you. You gave them such a wonderful gift when you healed them and you didn't take it back when they forgot about you. Thank you for your love. Please help US not to treat you like that. You give us many good things to enjoy. May we remember that they come from you. Help us to say thank you. Amen.

The leper—St. Matthew 8. 1–4

Lord Jesus, loving Saviour, Thank you for being so sure that you wanted to make the leper better. Thank you for being surprised that anyone could think you might not want to help him. Thank you for reaching out to touch him when everyone else was afraid to. We are glad that you are still the same today. Although we are not important in this world, we are to you. Thank you that you are always wanting to help us. Amen.

The woman who touched His hem—St. Mark 5. 24–34

Lord Jesus, we thank you that you were able to make the woman better even though the doctors couldn't. Thank you for healing her just through her touch. Help us to be sure, as she was, that when we reach out to you you will always help. Thank you that you are never too busy to hear. Amen.

The man at the Pool of Bethesda—St. John 5. 2–9

Loving Saviour, thank you that you care about those who have no one to help them. Thank you for finding the man at the pool and for knowing all about him. Thank you for making him better even when he had almost given up hope. Teach us to trust in you and to count on your help always, even when we feel like giving up.

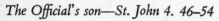

In your Name. Amen.

The Official's son—St. John 4. 46–54

We praise you, Lord Jesus, for you are the Son of God. You healed the boy in Capernaum when you were twenty miles away in Cana. We thank you that you are able to work wherever people are. Please make us like the boy's father, ready to believe that what you say is true, even when we cannot see it. Amen.

All who were brought—St. Mark 1. 32–34

We praise you, Lord Jesus, because you never leave anyone out. You healed *all* who were brought to you, however many there were, however late it was, and however tired you were. We thank you that today, too, you care for everyone who comes to you. Thank you for always having time for us. Amen.

THE LORD JESUS OUR TEACHER

The pearl of great price—St. Matthew 13. 45–46

Father God, may knowing you and belonging to your Kingdom become the most important part of our lives. Help us to be like the pearl collector in Jesus' story. May we be ready to put you first before everything else and, if some things have to go, help us to let them go gladly for the joy of knowing you.

In Jesus' Name. Amen.

The sower—St. Matthew 13. 1–9, 18–23

Heavenly Father, help us to hear what you say to us. Help us to believe you gladly and to obey you readily even when things are difficult. May we be like the good ground in Jesus' story, ready to hear your word and put it into practice, so that others may see your likeness growing in us.

For Jesus' sake. Amen.

The two sons and the vineyard—St. Matthew 21. 28–31

Please, Lord Jesus, teach us that *doing* things to help is more important than *saying* we will help. When people ask for our help, make us ready to say 'Yes' and even more ready to start at once. Help us to keep to our promises so that others may be able to count on us.

For your sake. Amen.

The unmerciful servant—St. Matthew 18. 23–35

Saviour Jesus, please help us not to be like the servant in the story—unready to forgive and unkind. You have forgiven us all our sins. You are so kind to us, even though we do not deserve it. Help us to be forgiving to the people we know, even when they do not deserve it.

Amen.

The good Samaritan—St. Luke 10. 25–37

Lord Jesus, please make us like the good Samaritan, always ready to stop and help when we come across someone in trouble. Make us ready to help even when we are busy or when it is someone we don't like very much or do not know.

We ask it because we want to be like you. Amen.

The Good Shepherd—St. John 10. 1–18

We are glad, Lord Jesus, that you are the Good Shepherd and we are your sheep. We thank you for taking care of us and being in charge of us. Thank you for knowing us by name. You have promised to lead us in the way we should go. Help us to follow you and keep close to you. Thank you for dying for us and coming alive again for us. Please teach us how to trust you more.

In your Name we pray. Amen.

The lost sheep and coin—St. Luke 15. 3–10

Thank you, Lord Jesus, for the happiness that comes from finding special things that have got lost. Thank you that we are special to you. Help us not to wander away from you by forgetting or disobeying you.

In your Name we ask. Amen.

The runaway son—St. Luke 15. 11–32

Father God, we love you because you have first loved us. We love you because you never stop loving us, even when we do not want to bother with your ways. We love you because, even though we don't deserve it, you are always ready and watching for us when we come to say sorry. We love you because your love never fails or fades away. Thank you for being like the father in Jesus' story.

Amen.

The runaway son's brother—St. Luke 15. 11–32

Please, God, help us not to be jealous and sulky like the elder brother in Jesus' story. Help us to enjoy all the wonderful things you give us. Make us ready and willing to share them with others, specially with those who do not know about you yet.

For Jesus' sake. Amen.

Sheep and goats—St. Matthew 25. 31–46

Lord Jesus, our Teacher, please help us to learn this lesson— that whatever we do for the least important person when they are in trouble, we do for you. Help us to remember, too, that when we refuse to help them it is the same as refusing to help you. Please give us caring hearts and make us loving in the little things we do, for you have said that even a cup of cold water given for your sake is a way of giving to you. Amen.

The two houses—St. Matthew 7. 24–27

Lord Jesus, please help us to be like the wise man who built his house on the rock. Help us to hear what you teach us, to listen to it carefully, to remember and obey it, so that when troubles and difficulties come along we shall be strong, knowing and depending on you. Amen.

The great supper—St. Luke 14. 15–24

We thank you, Heavenly Father, that you are like the King in Jesus' story. You have invited us to belong to your Kingdom and one day to be with you in heaven. Please help us not to make excuses. Help us not to be so busy and interested in the things around us that we do not want you.

For Jesus' sake. Amen.

THE LORD JESUS OUR KING

Lord over the earth

We praise you, Lord Jesus, for in the beginning you were with God making this world. Everything in it belongs to you. We praise you for calming the storm and walking on the water. We praise you for feeding five thousand people from one boy's picnic. We praise you for providing such a wonderful catch of fish for your disciples. We praise you for being in charge of the world today. Even now everything belongs to you. We are glad that one day everything will obey your voice. We praise you because you are the Lord. Amen.

Lord over the devils—St. Mark 5. 1–20

Lord Jesus, our King, we thank you that you didn't run away when the wild man came rushing at you. You were not afraid. We praise you because you are Lord over the devils. They have to do as you command. Thank you for setting the wild man free. Thank you that there is no need to be afraid when we know that you are with us. We praise you, Lord Jesus. Amen.

Lord over death—St. John 11 and St. Luke 8. 40–42, 49–56

We thank you, Lord Jesus, that you are Lord over death. You made Jairus' daughter come alive again even though the crowd laughed at you thinking it was impossible. You made Lazarus come alive again even after four days in the tomb. You are Lord over death, for you are God. We thank you that we do not need to be afraid of dying. We are glad that you are able to give us life like yours that never ends so that we may be with you in heaven for ever. We praise you, Lord Jesus. Amen.

40

THE
CHRISTIAN
YEAR

ADVENT

Lord Jesus, we thank you that long ago you came to our world as a baby to live and grow up and die for us. We thank you that you promised then to come back again one day as King to rule for ever. We thank you that you may be counted upon to keep your promise. Please teach us to live expecting you.

In your Name we pray. Amen.

Lord Jesus, our Saviour and King, we thank you that you have won the fight against Satan and sin. We thank you that when you come again you will put an end for ever to everything wicked and sad and painful. We thank you that you are coming with glory and power to settle once and for all the matter of right and wrong. Amen.

God, our Father, now that we are counting the shopping days to Christmas, help us not to be too busy or excited to remember that it is the birthday of the Lord Jesus. Help us to think of things to do that will please Him, and words to say that He would like to hear. Give us hearts that are truly thankful and minds that are ready to think about the words of the carols we sing.

For his sake we pray. Amen.

CHRISTMAS

Lord Jesus Christ, King of kings and Lord of lords, Son of God who made the world, we worship you today as the Baby of Bethlehem. We thank you for leaving heaven to be born as a baby like us. We thank you for growing up in a body like ours to show us what God is like. Amen.

God, our Father, we thank you for Christmas:
—for presents and postmen and parties and people to share our
    happiness with;
—for stockings and turkeys and crackers;
—for pantomimes and plays and special Christmas programmes
    on television.
You have given us all these things to enjoy. Please help us to remember that it is better to give than to get.

For Jesus' sake, who came the first Christmas to give himself to us. Amen.

We thank, you, Heavenly Father, for your present to us which is the greatest of all presents: the gift of your only Son, the Lord Jesus Christ, to be our Saviour. Amen.

Lord Jesus, this is your birthday. Help me to make it a happy one for you. Amen. *Last week*

Dear God, We did   *o sang our card.*

~~Heavenly Father~~, help us in our Nativity Play to show to others what a wonderful thing you did for us when you sent the Lord Jesus into our world. Help us to act and sing our best, *Thank you for helping* and through our play help us to understand more about the most important part of Christmas.

For Jesus' sake. Amen.

Lord Jesus Christ, you were pleased and ready to be made a baby. We pray this Christmastime for the babies of the world. Please bless them with your love and watch over their growing. Help their parents to bring them up in the truth of God's ways. Look after and heal those that are ill. Help those who live in places where you are not known. Send people to tell them, we pray, so that they, too, may have the chance of knowing you.

In your Name. Amen.

[*For Missionary Day (Epiphany) see 'Thy Kingdom Come'*]

ASH WEDNESDAY AND LENT

Lord Jesus Christ, you were tempted once like us. You know what it's like when thoughts of wrong things to do come into our minds. We thank you that you never did anything wrong. We thank you that you are able to keep us from doing wrong. Please help us when we are tempted.

In your Name we ask it. Amen.

Dear God, our Father, we want to be good followers of Jesus, doing and saying and thinking only those things that please you. Please teach us to want only the things you want, and to do and say and think only those things that you would.

For Jesus' sake. Amen.

Lord Jesus, when we have to choose between doing right or wrong, help us to choose right. When we have to choose between telling the truth or telling a lie, help us to choose the truth. When we have to decide between being unselfish or pleasing ourselves, help us to be unselfish.

For your sake we pray because we want to be like you. Amen.

PALM SUNDAY

We thank you, Heavenly Father, for the first Palm Sunday when you kept the promise you had made five hundred years before. Thank you for sending Jesus into Jerusalem riding on the donkey as a King. Thank you that the people recognised him and remembered your promise. Help us today to know that he is King and to remember that you always keep your promises.

In his Name. Amen.

Lord Jesus, Prince of Peace, we thank you that you went to Jerusalem as the King who goes in peace and friendliness. We thank you that you went there specially to die for us to make peace between God and ourselves. We thank you that because of what you did there we may be friends with God. And we thank you, too, that you come to us as the Friend who knows and loves us. Amen.

GOOD FRIDAY

Lord Jesus, you came into the world to take the punishment of our sins instead of us. You died in our place that we might go to heaven. Please help us to understand what a great thing it is that you have done for us. Help us to say thank you, thoughtfully, really meaning it.

In your Name. Amen.

Saviour Jesus, for loving us to the very end, we thank you.

For choosing of your own free will to die for us, we thank you.

For staying on the cross when you could have come down, we thank you.

For coming alive again to give us your strength and forgiveness, we thank you.

In your Name. Amen.

We thank you, Heavenly Father, for loving us so much that you gave the Lord Jesus to die for us. Thank you for sending him when he was your dearly loved only Son. You love us so much, Lord! Help us to love you back.

In Jesus' Name. Amen.

EASTER

Lord Jesus, our Saviour and Friend, we thank you that you are alive today, and though we cannot see you with our outside eyes, we may know that you are with us, for you have said, 'I will never leave you nor forsake you'. Thank you that we can say, 'The Lord is our helper; we will not be afraid'.

In your Name. Amen.

Lord Jesus Christ, we praise you. We are glad because of you, for you are the first to come alive to die no more. You have set us free from our sins by being killed for us. You are the living One who died and came alive again. We thank you that you are alive today and always. Amen.

O Lord God, thank you for looking after Jesus when he died and for using your great strength to make him come alive again. We are glad that you have given him a place beside you which is more special than any other place. Please help us to give him the first place in our lives. Please put your strength in us to make us strong to live for him.

For his sake. Amen.

Thank you, Lord Jesus, that you are living today. Thank you that every day you are loving me, teaching me, and hearing me when I pray. Help me to believe in my head and to know in my heart that you are with me. Amen.

We thank you, Lord Jesus, for coming alive again so that we may be strong with your strength to win the battle over sin. Amen.

ASCENSION

Lord Jesus, Son of God and Son of Man, we praise you.

For leaving your place in heaven to come as a man to earth, we thank you.

For finishing to the very end all that God sent you to do, we thank you.

For going back to your place of glory in heaven to pray for us, we thank you. Amen.

We thank you, Heavenly Father, that the Lord Jesus has made it possible for us to know you. Thank you that he sits at your side in glory. Thank you that he is making ready a place for us to be with you for ever. Thank you for giving him the highest place in heaven and the Name that is greater than every other name.

In the Name of Jesus we pray to you. Amen.

We thank you, Lord Jesus, that because you went back to God you were able to send your Holy Spirit to us. We thank you that you need not be just in one place at a time any more, but you are able to be with all your people all of the time. We thank you for being with us wherever we go.

In your Name. Amen.

WHITSUN

Dear Holy Spirit, you are the One who comes along beside us to help and comfort us. Please make us sure that you are with us. You are the Teacher who helps us to understand and remember what the Bible says. May we learn from you. You are God who comes to live in our hearts and love us. Help us to welcome you.

For Jesus' sake. Amen.

You have promised, Heavenly Father, to give the Holy Spirit to everyone who asks. Please give him to us. Send him into our lives to make us able to live for you. May he fill us and give us your love and gladness and make us like Jesus. Help us not to make him sad by anything we think or say or do.

For Jesus' sake. Amen

Please, Heavenly Father, help us to understand about the Holy Spirit. Help us to believe about him in our heads and know him in our hearts.

For Jesus' sake. Amen.

HARVEST

God, our Father, we have good things to eat that have come from all over the world: butter and ham and tea and oranges and lots of other things. Thank you that you are at work in all the world to give food to people everywhere. May they realise that these good things come from you, the living God.

In Jesus' Name. Amen.

Lord Jesus Christ, you have said that when we give food to the hungry and drink to the thirsty it is the same as giving it to you. We bring you now our Harvest presents. Please bless them and make them useful to the people who need them.

For your sake. Amen.

(For further prayers see, 'Give us this day our daily bread' Page 13. Prayers for a Bible Day can be found under, 'Thy Kingdom come' Page 8)

WHEN WE COME TOGETHER

Heavenly Father, thank you that you want to speak to us. Thank you for the Bible which is your message to us. Thank you for our . . . (Sunday school, etc.) where we can learn to understand the things you say. Please help us week by week to hear your voice more clearly. May we all, teachers and . . . (children) together, grow to know you better, obey you more quickly and love you more deeply.

In the Name of the Lord Jesus who died and rose again for us. Amen.

Lord Jesus Christ, you have said, 'Where two or three people come together in my Name, I am there with them'. Help us to be quiet now as we remember that you are with us here. Amen.

Father God, we have met together here to say sorry for the wrong things we have done. We have come to thank you for your love and kindness to us. We have come to tell you in our praise and song how great you are. We have come to hear and learn from your Word, the Bible. We have come to ask you for the things we need. Please bless us now and help us in our worship.

For Jesus' sake. Amen.

We thank you, dear God, that we don't have to be clever to understand the Bible, for you have promised to open our understanding so that we may know what you have said. Please do that for us today. Help us to remember what you teach us and make us able to obey it.

In Jesus' Name. Amen.

O Lord our God, you know what we are like inside, what we are thinking about and what we want. Please take over our thinking and our wanting now so that, forgetting about other things, we may want to think about you.

In Christ's Name. Amen.

The Church worldwide

O God our Father, we thank you that in every country in the world there are people who believe in you. We thank you that as we meet together here we belong to the great family of your people who are meeting together to praise you today. Thank you for making us one family in Jesus Christ. Thank you for making him the Head over us all. Please give us his love for one another. Help us to grow closer to him and to each other.

In his Name. Amen.

The persecuted Church

Lord Jesus, we are so glad to live in a country where we are allowed to come to church to meet with you. We are free to believe in you and to follow your ways. We can buy a Bible in almost any bookshop. We pray for those who cannot do these things. Please guard your people who have to meet in secret, and keep them safe. Help those who are in trouble for loving you. Please comfort them and make them strong and brave.

In Jesus' Name. Amen.

THE WORLD WE LIVE IN

THE WORLD WE LIVE IN

Dear God, thank you for pets, especially our own. Thank you for making them so beautifully. Thank you for the happiness they give us. Help us to look after them well and always to treat them as kindly as we like to be treated.

For Jesus' sake. Amen.

We thank you, O God, for the parrot and toucan, the leopard and lion. We thank you for the monkey and the polar bear, the turtle and koala. We thank you for the crocodile and hippopotamus, the antelope and llama. We thank you for filling the world with such interesting and beautiful animals. Help us to make sure that they have room to live and survive.

In Jesus' Name. Amen.

Dear God and Maker of the animals, we thank you for those that live on our farms and give so much for us. We thank you for the cow that gives its milk, the sheep that gives its wool, the hen that gives it eggs, and for all those that give us meat. We ask that the people looking after them may treat them kindly and with respect.

For Jesus' sake. Amen.

Loving God, you know when the smallest sparrow falls to the earth. We thank you that you love and care about the animals. We specially think today of all those that are ill or in pain. Thank you for the work of vets and veterinary nurses. Please guide them as they work to make the animals in their care well again.

In Jesus' Name we pray. Amen.

Heavenly Father, thank you for all the ways there are for us to learn about the animals you have made. Thank you for television programmes, films and books, for lessons in school and animals to keep and watch. Thank you that we may see the tadpole change into a frog, the caterpillar into a moth. Be with us in our learning. May we remember to praise you for the wonderful things you have made.

For Jesus' sake. Amen.

Dear God, we thank you for horses and the fun of riding. Please help us as we learn to ride to aim at the highest standards, to work hard, and to treat our ponies with thoughtfulness and care. Amen.

Creation

We thank you, Heavenly Father, for the beauty of the world that you have made: for gusty winds and red skies; for scurrying clouds and trees to climb; for daisies and dock leaves; for streams full of minnows and fields full of cows; for rivers and puddles and the sea with its crashing waves; for eyes to see and ears to hear; for skin to feel and legs to run. For making all these good things we thank you, Lord. Amen.

Morning

Thank you, Heavenly Father, for this new day. We ask you at its beginning to keep us from wrong. Whatever we do to-day may we do it the best we can as if we were doing it specially for you. Help us to share with others the kindness and gladness that you have given us. For Jesus' sake. Amen.

Evening

Lord Jesus, at the end of the day we come to thank you for all the good things we have enjoyed. We thank you, too, for giving us the night in which to sleep. Thank you for the beauty of the moon and stars, the comfort and cosiness of our beds. We pray for all who are troubled or homeless tonight and needing to know your love. Please help them. Lastly, we are sorry for the wrong things we have thought or said or done today. Please forgive us, Lord, and keep us safe while we are asleep.

In your Name we pray. Amen.

The seasons

Spring

Thank you, Heavenly Father, that you are making all things new again this Spring. Thank you for the song of the birds as they build new nests and look after their eggs. Thank you for new buds bursting into leaf on trees and bushes. Thank you for the fun of new things and for sharing this new Spring with us. Help us to share our new things, too.

For Jesus' sake. Amen.

Summer

Thank you, God, for the sunshiny days of Summer, for seaside holidays and games outside, for strawberries and ice-cream and gardens full of flowers. As we enjoy these Summer days we pray for those who find them difficult, specially those who are old or working in hot and noisy places.

In Jesus' Name. Amen.

Autumn

Heavenly Father, we praise you for the colours and scents of Autumn, for falling leaves and ripe fruits, for misty mornings and sunny afternoons. We praise you for the beauty of the countryside as it gets ready for Winter, and we thank you for providing the world with times for resting as well as growing.

In Jesus' Name. Amen.

Winter

O Lord our God, we thank you for the crispness of winter days and the fun of icicles and snow. Thank you for the sparkle of the stars on frosty nights, and the cosiness of winter evenings. We pray for those who are cold and underclothed and homeless.

Please help them, Lord, and please watch over those whose work is dangerous during winter.

In the Name of the Lord Jesus. Amen.

Space

We thank you, Lord, for the exciting adventures of spacemen and for all the new things they are discovering. Help us to learn the lessons they have learned: to be brave and adventurous —and obedient, too, just as they have to obey all that mission control tell them to do. Please keep them safe, Lord.

In Jesus' Name, Amen.

Machines and gadgets

We thank you, Heavenly Father, for all the machines and gadgets we have which help us and give us fun: for tape recorders, transistors and bicycles; for trains and cookers and heaters; for radar and television and satellites. Especially we thank you for the gadgets which help people who are ill to lead an ordinary life. We pray for our scientists that they may discover and invent things to help the world, not hurt it.

In Jesus' Name. Amen.

Our library

Thank you, God, for the fun of books, for stories and pictures and encyclopaedias. Thank you for our library and the people who work there for us. Please help us in our reading to choose good books and to treat them carefully.

In Jesus' Name. Amen.

Our school

Loving Father, may we remember that you are with us in school today. You know us each by name and all that happens to us. You know when we don't understand in the classroom and when we fall down in the playground. You have made our brains and our bodies. Please help us in our learning and in our growing—that our minds may understand and our bodies become strong.

In the Name of the Lord Jesus. Amen.

FOR MYSELF

FOR MYSELF

My birthday

Lord Jesus, today is my birthday. Thank you for the people who love me. Thank you for the cards and presents they have given me. Thank you for the special feeling that I have and for all the fun. Thank you for taking care of me through another year. I give this new one to you. Help me to grow more like you as the days go by. Amen.

When I am happy

Lord Jesus I'm happy today. I'm happy because . . . (*tell Him why*). Thank you for happiness and laughing and singing and jumping. Thank you for giving me this lovely feeling. Help me to share my happiness with others by thinking of them, too, and please comfort those who are sad today.

In your Name. Amen.

When I am feeling ordinary

Thank you, Father God, for all the ordinary days when I feel ordinary too. Thank you that feeling ordinary is really the same as feeling comfortable. You have given me all that I need. Thank you. Please help all those who are not so lucky as I am, specially children who are ill, hungry or cold.

For Jesus' sake. Amen.

When I have a difficulty
(*Tell God about your difficulty.*)

Thank you, Heavenly Father, that nothing is difficult to you. Thank you for promising to help me. Thank you for saying, 'Do not be afraid; I will help you'. Please help me with this difficulty.

In Jesus' Name. Amen.

When I am looking forward to something
(Tell God what you are looking forward to.)

Dear God, thank you for the fun of looking forward to things. Thank you for treats and exciting plans. Please may I be patient as I wait and help me not get too excited or silly as the time draws near. May it be a special time for everyone. May I remember to share my fun with you, too, knowing that you are with me in happy times as well as sad ones.

In Jesus' Name. Amen.

When I am afraid

Lord Jesus, I'm frightened. . . . *(tell Him why.)* Please help me to feel you close to me. Thank you that you are stronger than anything. Thank you that you are with me looking after me. Please take away my fear. Amen.

When I have to do something I don't want to do.
(Tell God what it is you don't want to do.)

Please, Father God, help me to be strong and brave to do this thing and able to do it with a smile. Help me not to make it difficult for others, too. Thank you that the Lord Jesus was even ready to die on the cross for me in spite of the pain. Please make me like him.

In his Name. Amen.

When I am disappointed

Loving Father God, I'm so disappointed because . . . . Please help me to be cheerful and not sulky. May I remember that you are loving me and with me just as much when I'm disappointed as when I'm happy. Amen.

When I am left out

Father God, I feel lonely and left out. Thank you that you haven't left me out. You promise always to remember me and never to forsake me. Thank you that I am important to you—but please help me to learn, too, how to let others come in front of me. Amen.

When I am sad

Heavenly Father, I'm sad because . . . Thank you for promising to comfort me as a mother comforts her children. Thank you for loving me. Please comfort me now.

In Jesus' Name. Amen.

When I have a secret worry

Lord Jesus, thank you that I can share my secrets with you and know that you will keep them. I am worried about . . . . You are God. You love me and promise to help me. Please sort out this worry for me. Now that I have given it to you please help me not to worry about it any more.

In your Name. Amen.

When someone has been unkind to me

Father God, you know what has happened. Please help me not to be angry. You forgive me the wrong things I do. Please help me to forgive . . . , too. Please take away my unloving thoughts and help me to think of ways to be friendly.

For Jesus' sake, who prayed for the people who were unkind to him. Amen.

When something terrible happens to me

Lord Jesus, I'm calling to you. Please help. Thank you that you are with me. You haven't changed. You are still looking after me and loving me. Help me to trust in you. Help me to feel you near me. Amen.

When I have been naughty
  (Tell God what you have done.)

Father God, I'm sorry for what I have done. I'm sorry for hurting others. Most of all I'm sorry for hurting you. Thank you that the Lord Jesus died to take away my sins. Please forgive me and make me clean again inside. Please help me not to do wrong.

In Jesus' Name I pray. Amen.

When I am ill

Lord Jesus, I am ill. Please make me well. Help me to be brave, and thankful to the people looking after me. Thank you for being here with me. Amen.

When someone I know dies

Thank you, Lord Jesus, that when we belong to you, dying isn't a dreadful thing any more. It is just the way we go to be with you in heaven, away from everything that hurts or scares or makes us sad. Thank you that it is only our bodies that die. Thank you that the real 'us' lives with you for ever.

Thank you, Lord Jesus, for knowing what it feels like to be sad when someone you love dies. You cried when your friend Lazarus died, even though you knew you were going to make him come alive again. Please comfort me now. Amen.

When I feel like giving up

Lord Jesus, I feel like giving up. Please help me not to. You can make me strong by coming into my life and being strong for me. Please do that now. You have said, 'Be strong and work, for I am with you'. Help me to keep going.

For my Mother and Father

Thank you, dear God, so much for ~~Daddy~~ *my* and Mummy. Thank you for the way ~~they~~ *she* love~~s~~ me and take~~s~~ care of me. ~~Thank you that I belong to them.~~ Please help ~~them~~ *her* with all the important things they have to decide and do. May they find out more and more how much you love them. Help me to show them by the things I do, that I love them, too.

For Jesus' sake. Amen.

For my brothers and sisters

Thank you, God, for my brothers and sisters. (*Tell God their names.*) Thank you for the fun of sharing and playing and living together. Thank you that they are so important to you. Thank you for looking after them, too. May we all grow up to know and follow you.

In Jesus' Name, who died and came alive again for us. Amen.

For my grandparents

Thank you, Heavenly Father, for my grandparents. (*Tell him about them.*) Thank you for the interest they take in me and all that they give me. Please help me to think of ways to make them happy. May they know that you are with them, caring for them and loving them all the time. Amen.

Aunts and uncles and cousins

(*Tell God their names.*)

Thank you, Father God, for my aunts and uncles and cousins. Thank you for their love and kindness to me. Thank you for all the fun of being in a family. Please keep them safe and teach them more about yourself. Help them to discover wonderful new things about you every day.

For Jesus' sake. Amen.

For myself

Father, what love you have given me that I should be called a child of yours! And so I am. Thank you for planning in love to make me your child through Jesus Christ. Help me to keep close to you.

In his Name. Amen.

When I want the Lord Jesus to be my Saviour

Lord Jesus, I've done lots of wrong things. I'm sorry. Thank you for dying on the cross for me. Please forgive me and take my sins away. I give myself to you. From now on I want to follow you and obey you. Please help me to get to know you. Amen.

INDEX

INDEX